ORDINARY MEETINGS *DON'T* INTEREST ME!

CREATIVE GROUP LEADERSHIP

BOOK 1

What Is Facilitation?

IWONA POLOWY

with Austin Wilson

Including stories from 25 Top Australian Facilitators

BOOK 1: WHAT IS FACILITATION?

Disclaimer

All of the information, techniques skills and concept contained within this publication are of the nature of general comment only, and are not in any way recommended as individual advice. The intent is to provide a variety of viewpoints. Should any reader choose to make use of information contained herein, this is their decision, and the contributors (and their companies) and authors do not assume any responsibilities whatsoever under any conditions or circumstances. It is recommended that the reader obtain his or her own independent advice.

All quotations remain the intellectual property of their respective originators. The Authors (publisher) do not assert any claim of copyright for individual quotations. While every effort was made to provide accurate contact details at the time of publication, the Authors do not assume any responsibility for errors, or for changes that occur after the publication, including third party websites and their content.

Edited by Kathryn Galán
Formatting by Wynnpix Productions, www.WynnpixProductions.com

National Library of Australia Cataloguing-in-Publication entry
Polowy, Iwona, 1980- author.
Ordinary meetings don't interest me : creative group leadership, book 1: what is facilitation? / Iwona Polowy with Austin Wilson.

ISBN: 9781533207067 (paperback)
Business meetings.
Group facilitation.
Leadership.
Conflict management.
Wilson, Austin, 1964- contributor
Creative group leadership
658.456

All enquiries, contact: hello@iwonapolowy.com
www.iwonapolowy.com
Perth, Australia

To all the people who have struggled
with ordinary meetings

###

ALSO IN THE CREATIVE GROUP LEADERSHIP SERIES

CONTENTS

CONTENTS

What People are saying about *Ordinary Meetings **Don't** Interest Me*

"*What is Facilitation?* is the must-have handbook before leading any group! Iwona and the 25 contributing facilitators have demystified the common understanding of facilitation ... and masterfully articulated the professional art that it is. Compulsory reading!"

> —Maree Wrack, Conversational Dynamics Specialist, Professional Speaker & Author
> www.upshiftsolutions.com.au

"Iwona and Austin have done a marvellous job in describing the leadership that process facilitators provide when they are on the job designing and guiding meetings. Indeed, the book highlights the value that facilitators bring to group situations by offering an alternate form of leading as they engage and consult groups about the paths they need and wish to go. Stories and quotes from real-life facilitators offer multi-dimensional perspectives that will be valuable for a more considered understanding about the field and profession of facilitation. Well done and I'm looking forward to the next book in the series already."

—Noel E K Tan, CPF
Trailblazer Associates International
www.go-trailblazer.com
International Association of Facilitators, Chair

"Iwona creatively uses the story of her own learning journey and quotes from some of Australia's top facilitators to develop a shared understanding about what facilitation actually does. It makes for compelling reading as the book brings alive what a facilitator (or process leader) is, their role and what the key ingredients are for a successful workshop. Read this book to find out why social intelligence and Sneaky Vegetables are essential to successful group processes!"

—Jackie Mundy,
Senior International Development
Consultant and Facilitator (CPF)

"Iwona is a "Process Leader" who lives and breathes facilitation. Together with Austin, they have written an easy to read book that can help experienced professionals and newcomers to facilitation. Her use of pertinent facilitation stories helped me to understand the variety of contexts and emotions that accompany this art. If you want some distinctions about what facilitation is and is not and how to do it better, I highly recommend you read this book."

—Tim Wise
Storytelling for Leaders
www.timwise.com.au

FOREWORD

This is a book about the power of facilitation - and what it takes to lift the capacity of groups of people to work together. However big or small the challenge, facilitation is the lever to use when the sledgehammer won't do.

I have been interested in facilitation for over thirty years of my professional working life as a change agent, as a consultant and as a leader in business and government. The stories in this book resonate with that experience and with a journey of self-discovery, I found myself on in learning the power of expert facilitation.

In my experience, good leaders understand the strength in the diversity of ideas that come from good facilitation. Great leaders go even further - they build a habit of using facilitation in all facets of what they do. They don't simply fall back on this at times of deep conflict. It works through-out the whole portfolio of leading: whether confirming a vision, planning a new business, setting scope for projects, engaging stakeholders or co-designing a product to name but a few.

When I was first introduced to the work of Peter Senge and *The Learning Organisation* in 1994, I was completely wrong-footed. Here was a management approach that challenged most of what I thought I knew. It said the smart guys in the room didn't have all the answers. In fact they didn't even know the right questions to ask. Here was a method that prioritised inquiry over advocacy, listening over persuasion, humility over ego. Here was the case for "Social Intelligence: to become part of the tool-kit of all leaders.

Fast-forward twenty years and Senge's case remains the same. Indeed, as people become less trusting and more cynical about leadership in business and government, the opportunity is even larger now and the need greater still.

As this book cogently argues, facilitators are Process Leaders who don't arbitrate the content. They have a client to serve but not at any cost. Their mission is to get real participation—and creating a safe environment for truth telling can only do this. The skill of a facilitator is to navigate this veritable minefield.

However, as this book shows, this is more than a set of skills and "techniques." It is about mindset, discipline and an approach. It's about reading other people and understanding context. And it's about relationships, which need to be built across workgroups and communities.

People collaborate effectively where there is a sense of trust—and this is where a good facilitator comes in!

—Philip Hind, Change Leader

INTRODUCTION

What an exciting time we live in!

The world of work is changing rapidly, putting more focus on people and on how we work together throughout our companies and supply chain.

Access to new processes, technologies, systems, the impact of globalisation, and myriad uncertainties enable each one of us to grow into new markets faster and to connect with more people, more organisations, and more communities than we ever could before.

Understanding how to work with groups of people so they can produce outstanding results has never been more challenging, nor more crucial to achieving success.

In the past, people used to sit in circles to talk through their issues of importance. Generally, there was a leader who set the tone for the meeting and who ensured that any decisions made were clarified and agreed upon by all.

Somehow, things have changed.

It's not only rare now to see people sitting in circles to have conversations, but it is also rare to have someone in discussions whose role it is to guide the group to achieve a good outcome.

A facilitator is someone who is not attached to an outcome or who has no need to interfere with the content of conversations. His or her whole interest is to bring people together to achieve an alignment.

Business nowadays has been far too slow to recognize facilitation as a methodology for change and to adopt it as a mechanism for needed transformation. Most of the time, facilitation is used as a complimentary skillset rather than as a stand-alone profession, like, for example, change or risk advisors or trainers. Over the past five years that I have been working as a facilitator, I have also noticed that the word "to facilitate" has evolved and how it is used for many different purposes that have nothing to do with the generic definition of facilitation.

The key to facilitation is being neutral in relationship to the content and having no vested interest in the outcome; this is the opposite of being "engaged," as most people may think is involved. Therefore, there is a distinct difference between facilitation, training, coaching, consulting, and being a master of ceremonies; the purpose of these roles is different, as we will cover in more depth, later in this book.

Words such as "to facilitate," "a facilitator," and "facilitation" became *fluffy* and lost their pure meaning. For example, I often hear:

CEOs saying, "I am facilitating positive relationships with other companies from our industry," meaning *I'm engaging with other companies;*

Managers saying, "I am a facilitator for my team when it comes to creating a plan for my department," meaning *I'm a group leader.* (You cannot facilitate your own group, as you have a vested interest in the planning.);

Trainers saying, "I've been applying facilitation with my students today, so they can learn more about the history," meaning *I have been teaching.* (When you teach, you have the responsibility for the outcome in a particular way; you apply a facilitative approach, but you are not a facilitator.);

My friend saying, "You need a facilitator for the marketing event," meaning *you need someone to MC the event;*

One of my clients saying, "A Facilitator means a scribe, doesn't it?" (A *Facilitator is not a scribe!*)

Why This Book is Important

Minds United, a not-for-profit organisation, conducted and published a survey in September 2012 that revealed that the vast majority of Australian-based facilitators are one-person companies; they find it hard to get clients and point at an urgent need to educate the public about the power of facilitation and the results available.

Despite many books available on such topics as facilitation, organizational development, conflict resolution, leadership, and those professional bodies set up to promote the profession, there is not enough *shared understanding* amongst leaders in business, government, and society in general about what facilitation actually does, and in particular the role of a facilitator.

If there was, I dare say that:

- More leaders in the world would make more progress with difficult conversations than in their past
- More teams would experience alignment, engagement, and motivation
- More organizations, regardless of size, location, or industry, could make more money, help more people, and do more good in the world
- More people would experience living fulfilled lives.

This book series addresses the *urgent need* to educate the public about the role of a facilitator and about facilitation in general and the ability of facilitators to help any group of people in their decision-making process to achieve better outcomes.

There are many aspects influencing the current confusion. These include:

INTRODUCTION

- Facilitators' own struggle to explain what they do in simple terms
- The use of abstract language that only confuses the public; and
- Lack of public information on how to access this profession.

Ours is not a profession you study at University; rather, it is something many people fall into, usually by chance. This contributes to the field not getting the recognition it deserves. Also, facilitators as a community are quite a hermetic group; they know how powerful their work is and yet often do not market themselves well. (Yes, there are some great exceptions)! The end result is fewer organizations accessing the tools and methods that can make a real difference for people, the workplace, and everyone's performance.

This series of books is important because they will:

- ➤ Address the language confusion, by re-defining the existing language and introducing the concept of Social Intelligence (SI)
- ➤ Provide a variety of lessons from inspiring facilitators/Process Leaders on developing group dynamics and the capacity for Social Intelligence

➤ Inspire, by sharing real case studies and outcomes achieved, particularly in Australia

➤ Give access to information about facilitation and facilitators in Australia and other regions in the world.

Without us all—the community of facilitators, clients, and the broader public—speaking the same language, there will never be the possibility for a true realisation of the benefits that arise out of people working together well. And there are many!

New Language

It's now time to introduce new language, starting with basic phrases such as:

- "Process Leader" instead of "facilitator"
- "Being Socially Intelligent" instead of "the facilitative approach"
- "Social Intelligence" in place of "facilitation"

Facilitators govern the workshop <u>process</u>, not the content. They do not try to steer their groups in any particular direction, nor do they provide any relevant content; rather, they design processes that match the group's intention, and they help the group go through the process, eventually coming up with an aligned approach. That is why calling them "Process Leaders" is more explicit and relevant.

Most groups, when working with someone who is a Process Leader, become more Socially Intelligent. That means they become more engaging by developing a greater awareness about themselves and others, and they expand their capacity to manage the social relationships within their group, which results in an enhanced ability to work together well. Clients, often called *sponsors* of those workshops, are influenced, too, by becoming more Socially Intelligent. A Process Leader works on "group intelligence" that affects each and every member, helping them to become more Socially Intelligent.

Intelligence is what you are born with, but Social Intelligence (SI) is mostly something that you have learned. Social Intelligence, *previously called Facilitation,* is defined as "the capacity to effectively navigate and manage complex social relationships and environments" (*Wikipedia).*

It takes effort and hard work to develop Social Intelligence, but this pays off in the end, in its benefits for your career and life.

The Journey begins

"The day came when the risk to remain tight in a bud was **more painful** than the risk it took to blossom."

~Anais Nin

BOOK 1: WHAT IS FACILITATION?

Initially, I loved it when someone would say, "You made it," as I climbed quickly to the top of what I could achieve as a Quality Assurance (QA) Specialist, working for oil and gas major contractor based in the UK. Just two years after Poland joined the EU, with a Polish degree in management and engineering, I was already working hand-in-hand with senior professionals from all around the world on complex engineering projects. I was very proud of my accomplishments.

My role was like that of a process auditor. It included planning, implementing, and auditing processes and management structures on projects. It seemed clear to me. Nevertheless, nobody—not my family or friends, not anyone outside of the industry actually knew what it was that I did.

In January 2010, the company I worked for announced redundancies. Over the next six months, over 700 people were made redundant, cutting thirty percent of their workforce. There were never enough people doing QA, however. Hence, my job was safe. But my bosses became sneaky. They started to use QA engineers like me to check up on people before they left. This did not feel right to me at the time.

I started to feel exhausted. I also stopped feeling that my work, including my written reports, was making anybody happy. In fact, I felt the opposite. That six-month redundancy-reduction period brought only more fear, uncertainty, and tears. Inside, I felt dissatisfied, disconnected, in conflict with my true nature, and in denial of the situation's reality. It took me a long time to see how I had created my own agony by escaping from who I really was.

For what? So I could go on impressing people I hardly knew?

And I did not even know this about myself. In fact, I did not know much about my person, either: not what my body needed, nothing much about my values and dreams, my likes and dislikes. From the moment I arrived to live in London, everything was rather accidental.

***

"This is not going to work," I said to my friend Ingrid, whom I often call Miss Livingontheboat.

We were having another glass of red wine in a cozy Notting Hill bar. I felt uncomfortable about writing down whatever dreams I had about my life, and I felt hopeless about my future. Somehow, though, she made me do it.

I surprised myself with what I wrote on that paper napkin: **happy; to be happy.**

I described images in my head, like blue sky, the sun shining, driving a car, people laughing, and feeling happy. I put down words like communication, platform, helping groups of people work together better, peace, happiness, and meditation; also, family and children. This exercise was liberating and somehow comforting. Still, for a long time, I did not share it with anyone.

But the flame had been lit. This exercise kick-started a journey of self-discovery that led me, in less than six months, to accept the job as a facilitator and trainer and move from Reading in the UK to Perth in Australia, one of the most isolated but also most beautiful cities in the world. Perth is a city of constant blue sky, the sun shining, driving in cars, and beautiful, happy people.

Yes, I was *that* damn lucky girl who got a sponsored visa and a job to live and work in Australia after just two phone calls! *They must like my heavy Polish accent,* I thought, as, at that time, I had no idea what the role of a workshop facilitator actually required.

However, I knew that I was already passionate about working with groups of people and helping them to achieve great results. I had a vision for transforming workplaces into places where people feel empowered, work together well, and are happy. That vision, which was created in a Notting Hill bar, is still alive, and it has become the drive behind all of my work initiatives.

***

For the last five years, I have worked as a facilitator with groups of people and diverse teams. In this book, I call this role a "Process Leader";

someone who designs and leads workshops that range from strategy to business planning, project framing to stakeholders engagement, decision-making, team alignment, and team building. I have worked mainly for Australian companies in the oil and gas industries, but also with entrepreneurs, artists, leadership teams in not-for-profits, Aboriginal communities, and government.

Now, you might be wondering:

How did I go from a process auditor to a Process Leader?

From setting up structures for improvement to supporting people in those structures so they can improve?

From analysing group results to helping groups to create outstanding results?

How did I switch my focus? And how can you?

Well, that's what this book is about. My core idea, however?

You've gotta be a Sneaky Vegetable first ☺!

If a young, Polish female with a distinct accent and experience wearing a quality-assurance hat, known for her expressive and often critical way of being, succeeded as a workshop facilitator by working, often with engineers and scientists, in the most blokey part of Australia—Perth—then you can do it, too!

If it was possible for me, it can be possible for you and for anyone else in the world.

I now feel more inspired and passionate than ever. I believe whole-heartedly that, with many others working in the facilitation field like me, a new generation of workers and leaders and group members will soon become "Socially Intelligent.". I can imagine now a future in which facilitators (what I call "Process Leaders") will commonly (rather than randomly) be used for problem solving and will regularly be called upon to help many more groups of people achieve outstanding results.

My Core Beliefs

This is what I have learned, based on my early years' experiences, and what I see as deep keys to personal and professional success and happiness:

- ❖ **Be true to yourself.** Keep checking in with yourself about what you do and how you do it. Tap into your feelings and emotions, not just into words.
- ❖ **Open up.** Don't be afraid to share your thoughts, including your frustrations, with someone you trust. But don't make it a constant complaint. Rather, use this as an opportunity for you to listen to your own voice.
- ❖ **Dream big.** Have the courage to write down what you really want, "as though it already happened": describe your feelings; feel free to draw or paint, if you are unsure of what you

want or how to put that into words. Don't
worry about the "how?" yet.

❖ **Accept opportunities.** Don't let any lack of
experience, knowledge, or language be a
barrier for achieving what you want. Have
courage and be more of "yes" person.

From Interviews to Book Series: How to Read the Creative Group Leadership Books

In the Australia-Asia region, there are two
distinct organisations that focus on sharing and
promoting the value of facilitation: the Australian-
Asian Facilitators Network (AFN); and the
International Association of Facilitators (IAF).

These organisations gathered some of the most
inspiring facilitators, whom we call here "Process
Leaders," and those who just complement their own
consulting toolkit. These are the leaders who are
transforming workplaces by applying their skillset to
help organisations create a culture of getting results
through collaboration. This series of books is a
celebration of this movement, particularly in
Australia.

The people interviewed for this series were
sourced mainly from the Australian-Asian
Facilitators Network group based in Australia/Asia/

New Zealand Regions, as well from my own contacts developed since moving to Perth in September 2010.

This book series contains lessons and experiences they have shared, in addition to their stories about trying to understand what facilitation is; about their journey of developing themselves; about working with clients and the challenges they've overcome; and real case studies from their work. The books also include examples of my own life lessons, which I share notably because I am someone who never set out to be a Process Leader. The books detail what it took for me to develop competency in this role.

Each and every person has been carefully selected for their inclusion based on client feedback, proven successes and great achievements, their reputation, and their willingness to collaborate on promoting the Process Leader as a profession.

This is the first book in the series. It focuses on helping the reader to understand what facilitation is and what it is not. In it, I introduce a new language that will be used throughout this book and later volumes, in order to make things clearer and more explicit.

The second book is about developing within you the skillset and experiences of a workshop Process Leader.

The third book is about understanding the common challenges in the field and how to deal with them.

INTRODUCTION

The fourth book offers case studies and outlines real, concrete benefits achieved by groups of people who have worked with a Process Leader.

The fifth book is about the future of facilitation, about creating collaborative workspaces, and what may come next.

Despite the fact that most people interviewed are Australians, the book is clearly applicable to and appropriate for use by those based around the world! As I've mentioned, I am a Polish woman who has worked in many different places and roles before having this job and writing this book. In order to develop this book series, it was extremely convenient for me to connect with professionals here in Australia, but I plan to expand the scope of this series and create similar projects based on the experiences of our fellow Process Leaders in Europe, Africa, Asia, and America.

I also encourage you to embrace confusion and uncertainty, as not everything will be revealed to you immediately. Such is the nature of emerging stories and case studies—it's often a case of "watch this space."

Also, these books are published as a series for a practical reason. It's easier to read that way, easier to pack if you are on the go, and beneficial to have some time and space between each book, in order to digest and reflect.

Please get in touch and let me know, after reading these books, what you've learned, what you are interested in now and what else you would like to focus on.

Read, get inspired, and connect.

Understanding What you Want

As a manager or leader, it is essential that you understand what you want both from the teams you work with and from your own organisation, including your own frustrations!

Have a look at the checklist below. If you tick any of the boxes, you may need a collaborative working culture and should consider working with a Process Leader!

- ✓ You and your team are looking for a clear and compelling vision and a plan
- ✓ You and your team are looking for new solutions to a new or existing problem, and more than one perspective is needed
- ✓ You and your team are looking to have an open and honest conversation about something that has happened
- ✓ You and your team are looking for a new strategy plan as a result of a change
- ✓ You and your team want to frame an opportunity, an initiative, or an idea
- ✓ You and your team want to better understand a complex issue wherein different people hold different parts of the puzzle or have different expertise

INTRODUCTION

✓ You and your stakeholders are looking for common ground in order to develop good partnerships with other stakeholders

✓ You and your stakeholders are looking for new ways to achieve better results

✓ You and your stakeholders are about to make an important decision

✓ You want more results and better relationships.

And it's more than that!

Have you become frustrated with your organization's current focus on profit? Are you now looking for new ways to do more good and make a bigger difference in the world?

Or are you already quite Socially Intelligent and now want to focus on doing something about which you are really passionate, so that you can really enjoy your work and the people?

Now, I am not suggesting that you all run out and quit your jobs! Rather, I invite you to take the ideas in this book and the other books in this series, and use them to turn your workplace into a positive, inspirational, and happy place for people to be in every day.

Who knows? Being Socially Intelligent might inspire you!

So don't wait and set your goals! Writing your goals and knowing the outcome helps your mind focus on finding the information you need. The process helps to ensure that the time you spend is worthwhile.

Start by answering these questions:

- What are you expecting out of reading this first book?

  _____

  _____

  _____

  _____

  _____

- What challenges can you already identify with your team or other people you work with?

  _____

  _____

  _____

  _____

  _____

- What benefits do you think might arise from people working well together?

  _____

  _____

  _____

  _____

  _____

CHAPTER 1

SOCIALLY INTELLIGENT APPROACH (SIA)

Most people get confused between the role of a facilitator and having a facilitative approach.

So I am going to start by explaining the facilitative approach. This is what we call a **Socially Intelligent Approach (SIA).**

And here is where the story really begins....

"Obviously, people want social calm, but if you do not let clever and ingenious people to participate, obviously there must be some dormant volcano that will erupt, sooner or later."

—Lech Walesa,
Founder of the social movement and first Polish
Trade Union Party, "Solidarity,"
which aimed to better the lives of workers and
drive social and economic change.

***

I was born under the communist system in Eastern Europe, during times when the "collective interest" of the people was determined not by the people themselves, but by the communist party, and was often aimed against individual rights. It was a system under which people felt suppressed; they had limited freedom of speech, press, and assembly.

Everyday life was made up of the same daily and weekly routines; it offered similar opportunities and experiences to everyone. For ordinary people who lived in Communist Eastern Europe, a large part of everyday life consisted of searching and waiting for basic material goods including food; and standing hours each day in long lines in order to purchase meat and potatoes, due to the frequent shortages of food, as well as personal hygiene and health items, including toilet paper, feminine products, and medicine.

I often saw very little of my parents. They were away from home each day for long stretches of time, working and shopping for basic necessities. They learned to be strategic about those food-shopping lines, in order to get things done on time and bring food home.

Like most of the children born in the PPR (the Polish People's Republic), I remember that the meals served to us in nurseries and kindergartens were a real nightmare. For breakfast, it was semolina and burnt milk with a skin formed on top, or it was milk soups with overcooked noodles and, of course, milk skin. There were noodles with cottage cheese, "lazy" dumplings (which had cottage cheese mixed into the dough) with breadcrumbs, rice with cream and overcooked apples, or racuchy (a kind of pancake or sweet fritter, often with apple inside). Everything was abundantly sprinkled with lots of sugar and wheat.

During meals, especially in kindergarten, we were forced to eat everything on our plate, including a liquid jelly or pudding desserts. The food was meant to be nutritious, and everyone was supposed to eat "properly."

Life was not so easy for a child like me, as I was born with food allergies to gluten, dairy, and wheat; I also had an aversion to meat. At that time in Poland, nobody really knew anything about allergies, so it took years for my parents to discover what stopped me from eating and what caused my vomiting.

You wouldn't believe how sneaky my parents had to be to get me to eat almost anything!

While most people under the communist systems of Eastern Europe ate in canteens and "milk bars," my parents became inventive and sneaky in their home cooking, given the economic situation. Cabbage, root vegetables, parsley, dill, and wheat (all sorts of wheat products) dominated our markets and greengrocers. I did not like most of these products, in addition to meat.

Things got a bit easier when my mum decided to involve me in making my own food. Suddenly, my experience of vegetables changed. As it became my own experience, I started to love it. I never did return to eating meat, but I managed to learn different ways to cook vegetables and fish and to prepare a variety of fruits.

"When adults, like children, are involved in finding solutions to their own issues, challenges, and concerns, suddenly their experience of those challenges changes", as much as their experience of participating in a facilitated workshop, and they usually love it.

I used to secretly call my mum a "Sneaky Vegetable," as she had a unique approach to getting the most stubborn person I ever met—*me!*—to eat vegetables. She was successful by applying just these simple rules:

1. **Create an experience**. I didn't know what I didn't know. Kids eat what they know and won't ask for a special meal if they do not know it is an option.
2. **Make fun.** She let me play with the food on my plate, which included applying sequences to eating and colour coding that made food look yummy. By relating healthy food to fun things that a child already loves and by turning mealtime into a game, she found a great way to get a few bites down the hatch.

3. **Involve.** I loved when she let me help her cook, even if it was just peeling a few carrots. She also praised me a lot, both during and at the end of cooking together.

4. **Don't force the finish.** Negative food experiences have the opposite effect of what's desired and actually increase or reinforce the tendencies of picky eating. "Require one bite but try not to start a fight" was her motto. At the same time, I was finally accepted as someone who would not eat meat.

Later, when I reflected on my childhood, I saw how quickly I learned the *power of involvement.* In my family, this meant becoming involved with creating my own food; in my country of Poland, it was discovering the power that came from involving people to attain their own freedom of choice. Throughout my childhood and teenage years, Poland underwent constant change. Change was anticipated for years; it was something that everyone looked forward to, as the path to real freedom and social and economic happiness. Involvement through the "Solidarity Movement" was a natural mass response to what was happening.

"The sole and basic source of our strength is the solidarity of workers, peasants and the intelligentsia, the solidarity of the nation, the

solidarity of people who seek to live in dignity, truth, and in harmony with their conscience. We hold our heads high, despite the price we have paid, because freedom is priceless."

—Lech Walesa

Hence, there is something of the warrior in me.

For as long as I can remember, all I wanted for myself and others was the freedom to choose the *what*, the *how*, the *where*, the *who* with, and the *when* without the pressure of other people telling me what to do, and I have always been prepared to work hard to get it. I also learned that involvement is one of the ways to bring other people on a journey with you, which means that you actually get more out of what you want, anyway.

When I moved to my university city, Wroclaw, to study for my master's degree in engineering and management, I was not as interested in the *content* of my study as I was in the social aspect of people coming together. For this reason, I joined a number of student associations, including "Wiggor," where I had a chance to design my own project... something I loved doing.

My favourite project was to design and manage a three-day music festival in the city centre that would connect students from all different universities and showcase a variety of different music styles, from jazz to rock, from indie to groove. Thanks to some generous sponsorship, we were able to invite musicians to attend from all over the country.

I was the MC for the event, so I stood on the stage at the front of the club, before hundreds of people drinking and dancing like crazy, and I told them all kind of stories to make them laugh. I even stood next to one of the most popular rock singers in Poland, and, initially, I was close to a meltdown. Yet something inside me *loved* doing this. I don't remember a single word I said, but when I saw so many people happy and smiling at me, I felt like I was doing something good; I felt connected, and there was magical energy in the room. I loved that energy, and I wanted to stay in that moment forever.

One thing I really loved learning about when at university was what makes one company win over another. Why do some organisations perform better than others? What makes a real difference in getting recognised in the world?

I only knew information from books plus my own observations of small Polish businesses, which did not amount to much. Hence, I was hungry for stories about achieving world-class organisational and team performance. This led me into setting up the Quality Management Students Organisation. Our aim was to go to businesses and find out what worked and what didn't, in implementing quality management systems standards based on international requirements.

I had about ten students who worked with me on a yearlong project that involved surveying small- and medium-sized organisations in the area, so that we could publish a research book based on their experiences implementing ISO 9001 requirements. Then we organised a conference with reps. from the government to show them the results and share with them factors that helped achieve organisational sustainability and competitive advantage.

None of us had much knowledge about the content at the time. We had no business connections, no budget, and limited access to computers, Internet, or phones. There was no Facebook and other social media, either, hence there were limited ways to replicate some defined ways of working.

I had a dream of what I wanted to see happening in that year. I also knew I wanted the survey to culminate in a big event. I knew I needed to get people really involved and let them take on roles that they were excited about.

I managed to convince the team to go away for a three-day weekend, stay at cheap backpacker hostels, and get to know each other (which often involved drinking large amounts of alcohol). Together, we created the vision for what we wanted to happen during the one-year timeframe and what our plan was going forward.

One day, I would read an article about something called strategic planning, and the very next thing I did was play that out with the group.

Once, we all sat together on the floor, and I asked people to write down a story about the project that they wanted to read about in the national newspaper once the project was complete. I asked them how they wanted to feel about it, what they would be acknowledged for having done, and what difference it would make to them and the world. We then read those stories aloud. Everyone was inspired by and excited about these opportunities to learn new things together and by participating in a project that would be so successful and published in the media.

It was clear that, once we had a common dream, things got a lot easier.

As a result, we learned heaps about the content. In addition, most of us got offered jobs in well-known organisations. The paper got published, and a local newspaper and radio station covered the story. Everyone felt accomplished and happy, and I became a master at leading enrolment conversations.

***

Here is what I have learned from my early years' experiences:

- ❖ People want social calm
- ❖ People have expectations. People expect transparency, genuineness and space to share their thoughts, feelings, desires and motivations

❖ People want relationships. People need to feel valued, safe and appreciated for their contribution, abilities and roles as opposed to being used, ignored or undervalued

❖ By letting people participate you help them to create a shared experience and understanding

❖ People want clarity, explained decisions and trust, hence having one common vision for the group makes things easier

❖ People need to feel like they have permission to make their own choices in life and are capable of making them.

Whether you live in a Soviet country, lead a group of students at a University or a government party, in order to work with large numbers of people effectively and to get them to do incredible things, you need to develop a certain kind of approach.

What approach do you need when working with people?

The meaning of Socially Intelligent Approach (SIA)

"Approach" here means the way you look at the world, at yourself in the world, at the people in the world, and at what you are trying to achieve in this world. Depending on your approach, you could create fear, disgust, hatred, and conflict OR generate love, rapport, empathy, and understanding within your relationships.

It is the *approach* that can either make you do "big things" or put you or other people down.

You also need relationships in order to feel safe, and you need to feel safe in order to feel happy, and feeling happy is *very* important if you wish to have a satisfying and fulfilling life.

If you want better-quality relationships but are wondering how difficult it will be to change, or if you are thinking you are too old or stuck in your ways to change, or even if you think you're not good at these "soft skills," think again!

The brain is very plastic; in other words, it's totally capable of learning new ways of operating and connecting. There's no reason whatsoever that you can't also learn to be more emotionally and socially intelligent. All humans can!

The **Socially Intelligent Approach** means being able to understand social situations, "read" other people's behaviour, and use your skills and intuition in appropriate ways.

Scientists have explored the concept of "Social Intelligence" for nearly 100 years, with the original definition being "the ability to understand and manage men and women, boys and girls, to act wisely in human relations" (Thorndike, E.L., 1920).

One of the better-known leaders in this area is Daniel Goleman, who has studied the brain and emotions and, in his studies, explains that Social Intelligence is about understanding how the brain works, what its triggers for reaction are, and how these can be enhanced or, in some cases, changed. This is where recognizing that you can "rewire" the brain and get it to work more effectively is very important, and that, as you learn to do this, you become more Socially Intelligent and vice versa.

It's important to note that emotional and Social Intelligence are very different from simple intelligence. In fact, much of the previous findings on intelligence and, namely, intelligence quotient (IQ) tests have been proved to be flawed. Which means not every person with a high level of IQ finds it easy to thrive in social environments; often, they feel quite opposite.

For some, Social Intelligence is common sense. For others, it's a learned way of being that can be developed and becomes a foundation for your work as Process Leader.

A Sneaky Vegetable

Don't take this the wrong way! "Sneaky Vegetable" is not just like any other "sneaky" thing, and it has nothing to do with being sly, dishonest, nasty, unreliable, or double-dealing. Like my mum, who used to work with me to engage me in eating more vegetables and fruits, a **Sneaky Vegetable** is *someone who can demonstrate a particular way of being, plus techniques and skills, usually with a whole group of people, in order to get more out of what the group really wants.*

When working with a group, however, a Sneaky Vegetable is intentional, but not obvious in the ways they apply their strategies, tricks, or engagement methods, and they avoid explaining too much—hence, he or she is actually sneaky.

Their key objective is to keep a group working on what that group wants to achieve, not focusing on the process being applied for them to do their work. On the other hand, if the process is not working, it does need to be changed to something that can better help the group and not slow the thinking process.

A Process Leader constantly seeks new avenues to expand to a higher level of Social Intelligence by bringing to bear this Sneaky Vegetable approach.

Applying the Socially Intelligent Approach (SIA)

The SIA can be applied by anyone in any context, environment, or social situation. It is a foundation platform to work from for the Process Leader as well as for a trainer, teacher, coach, consultant, or someone who is emceeing an event, including a scribe!

"In training, for example, we often use a facilitative approach (SIA) as opposed to facilitation (Social Intelligence)," says Amrit Kendrick.

"I guess many people exhibit SIA. So, for example, if you have a group of friends trying to make a decision, you might have one person who just naturally asks the quiet person what they think. Or someone who just naturally clarifies by saying, 'So, we've been talking about whether we should go on holiday to Bali or Down South,' and then they might summarise some of the main concerns that have been brought up about each option," Claire Vanderplank.

How to Recognize Someone with a Socially Intelligent Approach

There are some essentials of the SIA. These include:

- Connects easily with people from diverse backgrounds. It's often due to their excellent capacity to listen and speak up.
- Knows what matters most—kind of the Think Global/Act Local approach; including knowledge of relevant social rules, norms, and habits.
- Listens and invites more questions in order to get people to speak up and participate in conversation.
- Able to listen beyond the norm in such a way that people feel understood and valued.
- Flexible, and able to make quick decisions or change plans, if need be.

How to Develop the Socially Intelligent Approach

It takes time and hard work but it is possible!

More on this topic will be described in the second book in this series, but you can start with the following:

- ❖ Pay attention to the social world around you, including your own feelings, emotions, and behaviours
- ❖ Work on your communication skills, including listening
- ❖ Start asking questions that matter
- ❖ Practice "active listening" by reflecting back what the speaker has said
- ❖ Learn from your successes and failures.

In summary, here are the key points to remember:

- ✓ Socially Intelligent Approach is a foundation for your work as a Process Leader, trainer, coach, mediator, or MC of an event
- ✓ Being a Sneaky Vegetable is about the way you work with groups so they produce outstanding results without the need to focus on the process
- ✓ You can develop Socially Intelligent Approach for yourself and for others!

Before you move on to reading the next chapter, please reflect upon the Socially Intelligent Approach. Write down your own answers to the following questions:

1. **What is the role of a Process Leader?**

_____

_____

_____

_____

_____

_____

2. **What is Social Intelligence?**

_____

_____

_____

_____

_____

_____

CHAPTER 2

THE ROLE OF A PROCESS LEADER

So, what is the actual role of a facilitator, which I call here a Process Leader?

Is the role similar to that of a trainer, a coach, a moderator, or an event coordinator?

If not, what's different? What do other people say?

Is it all about telling people what to do?

***

I got the job as a facilitator and trainer after just two phone calls, and I immediately moved from Reading in the UK to Perth, Australia with all of my expenses covered by the organisation. All I knew about the job was that it required running workshops and frequently standing up in front of people to help them with project planning.

I knew I could do it, and, more importantly, I knew I'd love to run workshops and get paid to tell people what to do or tell them off, if they were not doing what I told them to do!

I saw it as a perfect transition, from quality checker to Process Leader ... getting paid to tell people what to do and in what way.

That was how I perceived the job when I applied for it. At the time, I thought I must be right, as I was awarded the job, along with two years' sponsored visa, all expenses paid, plus free accommodation, and car for a month. It was more than I'd ever asked for.

Even so, it was hard to accept this offer, in part because I had three others on the table. One offer was to work in Oslo, Norway, and initially it seemed very exciting. It was also the best financial proposition. The major difference was that all of the offers, other than that from Australia, were to continue working as a quality assurance specialist.

"You can choose what you want," said my friend Ingrid, when we were sitting on her boat one Sunday afternoon. "But how long do you want to do what you don't like doing?"

"The numbers say you should go to Norway," said another friend who was crunching the job offers for me to help clarify the actual benefits. "Besides, it's still in Europe, so it will be a lot easier to stay in touch with friends and family."

That evening, I found myself sitting on the floor, pretending to meditate (which I had never done before) and asking God for answers.

Soon, it was clear that my heart and soul were ready for new adventures in my life. It was difficult to leap, however, as all of my treasured friends and family wanted me to stay in Europe. Still, the earlier unspoken desire of working with groups of people had already been born. It felt right. It was like a calling to drop my existing way of life and seek new ways of self-expression.

Was I ready? Probably not.

Did I get prepared? I didn't know how.

I had been told that, if I went to Australia, I would have a mentor to work with for a while, but I still had no clear idea what facilitation was about and had never met a facilitator before.

Difficult Conversations

There were about ten people sitting in the room. Anticipating. It was my first time I was leading a workshop.

They had come together to review what had actually gone well on the project and to analyse what had not gone as well as they would have liked. We call it a "lessons learned" workshop.

It started well. When they all got into brainstorming what had not gone very well, I noticed several Post-it notes on a large white sheet of paper with the comment *"bullying."* I was stunned and did not know what to say.

I pointed to those notes then read them aloud and asked if this was a topic people wanted to talk about. To my surprise, a few nodded their heads. I looked at them again, in case they changed their mind, but they did not. I started by acknowledging them for their courage and said I had neither experience nor knowledge of how to have those conversations. I suggested we park that issue and follow up using a formal organisational process.

Later, I beat myself up for what I'd done. Or, more specifically, for what I *didn't* do. This was an ideal opportunity to get into a real conversation that mattered. Unfortunately, no one raised these issues later through any formal process. They'd chosen to open up in my workshop, but I hadn't had the strength in those areas to help them out. I felt powerless, as though I had let them down.

"It was not your role to do anything," my mentor told me afterwards. "You did okay."

And I knew he was right. I knew by then that my role was to work with a group of people in order to help them achieve whatever objectives they set. But part of me still really wanted to *help* this group of people. I'd believed I could and, if something happened in my workshop, I wanted to be able to deal with it.

Leading a process has an impact on the content, the environment, and the people, not just the process and objectives themselves.

So I started to wonder: what is in my scope of work and what is not?

I was beginning to discover that it's simply not my job to deal with the impact or outcomes of the workshop. It is more about empowering people to deal with their impacts, themselves.

Facilitating Workshops in Your Area of Specialty

Our QA department was going through a number of changes, and I was asked to facilitate conversations around the change process. Because of the hat I had worn previously, as a QA specialist, I found myself very comfortable with the nature of this problem, and I thought I knew what the team was trying to achieve.

I've done this before, and I know the path to follow, I thought to myself, secretly seeking confirmation from the team.

So I was surprised when they did not like the idea; the more they questioned international standards, the more astonished I became. I thought, *These Aussies are not getting it. They're not going to adopt it as their way.*

Later in the workshop, I discovered that this judgment in my head was getting in the way of my actually listening to them with my full attention. The group did the plan as best they could, but I was left feeling very tired, with no energy and even a little bit of resentment toward them for choosing the other direction.

***

It is still okay to facilitate a workshop in your own area of expertise, but it requires extra focus and ability to "park" or put aside all of what you know and think about what the group should or should not do. You also must be hyperaware of the impact of what you do and don't say, in order to give the group total freedom to make choices for themselves.

My first few months of working as a Process Leader were full of insights about myself and about the role of being a Process Leader. I learned that being a Process Leader:

- ❖ Is not about analysing and criticizing people
- ❖ Is not about telling people what to do
- ❖ Requires greater understanding of yourself and others

***

The Standard Definition

A dictionary definition of "to facilitate" is to make things easier, to assist in the progress.

The International Association of Facilitators (IAF) defines a "Process Leader (facilitator)" as "someone who plays an impartial role in helping groups become more effective. They should assume responsibility for the group processes, and they should not apply content expertise. They have no vested interest in the outcome, whether to be a financial gain or not."

A Process Leader versus Trainer, Teacher, Coach, Mediator and MC

What do these various roles and titles have in common?

They can all apply a Socially Intelligent Approach and be Sneaky Vegetables.

However, "there are important differences between the role of a Process Leader, coach, trainer or a teacher, a moderator, MC, **because their purpose is different.** These terms are often used interchangeably, which causes again confusion" *(Facilitating with Ease,* Ingrid Bens*).*

While many people in the workplace think and regard themselves as Process Leaders, the truth is that they probably aren't—not in the same sense as I mean, where a Process Leader works to develop a social intelligence in a group environment. They might be teaching, motivating, or providing resources to make things happen, however.

So what are the differences between the Process Leader versus trainer or a teacher, coach, mediator, moderator, or MC of an event?

Process Leader versus Trainer or Teacher

Jeremy Lu says: "So, from a teaching, training, and learning perspective, there's always imparting knowledge. You're always presenting information and getting students to critically analyse it, think about it, then you give feedback and test their understanding. That's the teaching side.

"When you are being a Process Leader, on the other hand, you're actually sensing, observing, and guiding. So there are two very different roles. When I play the head Process Leader, my role is not necessarily to share what I know or tell them what I think. In fact, you have to turn that part of your brain off.

It's more about questioning their thinking. Getting them to share their opinion. Getting them to see and appreciate thoughts from each other and then leading them."

Process leader does not teach anything.

Process Leader versus a Coach

Cindy Tonkin says: "Coaching for me is about where an individual wants to go. Process leader is about where a group needs to go or wants to go. And then training is essentially, 'Let's deliver some outcomes of knowledge.' So, we might have knowledge as an outcome, but it could purely be 'we need to bond' or 'we need to explore our options' or 'we need to understand our strengths.' Process leader role is a group thing. I consider the skills to be complementary, but they are not the same thing."

Process Leader versus a Mediator

Alan Halford says: "Mediation is when people talk about conflict resolution, and you are considered an expert at being objective. I use a mediation process, which is anything but objective, because, if you are in the room with two other parties or ten other people, the fact that you are in that room means that you are influencing what is happening, so how can you be objective?

"When I work as a Process Leader, using for example an Open Space method, there is no difference to what I am working with as a mediator. It is on the same continuum. Sometimes mediation is very formal, and sometimes it is sitting around, having a cup of coffee, but it is the same process—it's a dialogical process, where the person who is the Process Leader does not set the agenda, does not decide what happens. The people involved decide what happens. I think that is an important thing."

Process Leader versus a Moderator

"A moderator is someone who leads a meeting, forum, or discussion, who oversees the communication activities and is allowed to apply the knowledge ('content') to help the progress and directions of the conversation." (*Facilitating with Ease,* Ingrid Bens*)*

Process Leader versus-Event MC

"MC—Master of Ceremony or of a Conference— Someone who leads a ceremony or a conference-type gathering to have the event be well organized; is often there to entertain the audience." (*Facilitating with Ease*, Ingrid Bens)

Process—Leader enables the energy to be created by the group.

Jill Chivers says: "One of the things that differentiates a Process Leader-led event is where the energy is. The energy should always be with the group; the Process Leader is often outside of the energy of the group. So, that can be the co-ordination role of the travel guide, in a way. That is also what makes it different from a presentation, where the energy is with the person on the stage or from a training, where the energy moves from the person delivering the content, the expert, through to the students, who are assumed to have a lesser or lower degree of knowledge."

As Seen by Other Facilitators (ASOF)

Process Leader is someone who works with the group to achieve their goal.

Janet Rice says: "For me, the role of Process Leader is someone who works with a group to achieve their goals. Focuses on the process to allow the group to maintain their focus on the content. So, it's about helping to keep the group on track, making sure that everybody in the group is participating and is able to contribute, and supporting people in the group, if things get tricky and there are some conflicts and differences."

Process knows how groups of people operate.

Amrit Kendrick says: "For me, it is someone who knows how groups of people operate. They are skilled in getting the best out of the group, as they have a series of techniques and methods that allow them to work with people regardless of education, cultural background, or gender. They organise a program for that group of people to step into, that allows each of them to be engaged, to express themselves, and to feel that their input is valued in that setting."

"A Process Leader is someone who finds what works for a given group of people and then has them talking together and listening to each other."—Amrit Kendrick

Process Leader helps getting people to where they are heading.

Cindy Tonkin says: "It is not about getting people head-on, but rather understanding where people are heading to and working with them to get them to the outcome that is appropriate—whether it be an outcome the client has specified or an outcome that the client wants for themselves."

Process Leader is cleaning up messes.

Cheryl Gilroy says: "You can do damage to people by hearing people, taking them seriously, and then doing nothing. Process Leaders have an enormous responsibility, and a large part of my job is cleaning up messes. And cleaning up messes of when people have come forward with their great ideas or their concerns or their issues, and they think they have been heard, but they haven't because nothing has happened. For me, I have the reputation (which I really used to dislike, but now I like) of, 'If you have the angriest, crankiest, most pissed-off group, call Cheryl Gilroy, because she will come and clean it up.' I used to find that quite insulting, that I would go into all these furious groups, but I have actually found, over the years, that, as long as they are angry—which is fantastic; that is passion—we could turn that into something."

Process Leader in a workshop is a very cool space to be.

Chantal Harris says: "For me, the Process Leader in a workshop is a very cool space to be in, in terms of working towards some kind of outcome or some kind of new thought or for creating an idea. So, during the process of leading a group, you experience the way other people look at things or really focus on some kind of process or some kind of way things are done, but you are adding new ideas.

"You are almost looking at things from underneath, picking it up and turning it around and playing with ideas and bringing other people's perspectives into that. You may see something yourself, and the person next to you may look at the same thing and see something completely different, so, all of a sudden, through the role of a Process Leader, people can start to have insights into how you think about things and start to see things a bit differently. It's much more of an interactive exchange of knowledge—it's the opposite of something where the exchange of information is one-way, like, say, a lecture at university."

"A Process Leader makes everything very interactive and needs to blend all the experiences and knowledge of everyone in the room into a new idea or something workable for the group."

Process Leader brings a process to a gathering of people.

Rick Sommerford says: "It is about bringing a process to a gathering of people. It is also about giving others a method by which they might reach their goals. In that way, it is something along the lines of 'to make easy' for groups of people, in particular. When you act as a Process Leader for their goals, you give people a format they can use to get there."

Every ship needs a rudder.

Jeremy Lu says: "The way I think about it is that every ship needs a rudder. Sometimes you need more than one rudder. And it needs a direction.

Facilitation is about getting the right people onto that ship. And then helping them set a course or determine where they want to head towards.

"And then the Process Leader's role is of being that rudder, which is a very small piece of the entire object. You know one person in a big organization, but that rudder just helps guide the journey and the destination, to try and make it as smooth and as efficient as possible."

"Well, I'm lucky in the tax office I work," says Nick Housego. "Most people know the meaning of facilitation. But when we get externals in—people from outside business looking into the organization, or assisting us with co-designing and collaborating on projects, they may not necessarily know what a facilitator does.

"They certainly don't know what a good process facilitator does. Facilitators really have to know what's got to be achieved and how to develop a process to make that happen with the group.

"Most of the groups in the workshops that I have are subject matter experts. They've got particular skills relevant to their area. And my skillset is to ensure their voices get surfaced, get talked about; that their ideas get made visible by going onto the butcher's paper or the whiteboards.

"And then we start drawing understandings together of what we're seeing going up on the visual. So it makes a big difference with a facilitator in the room. It allows people to feel safe about discussing things. The environment's safe. I'm objective. I don't know your business. So you can tell me stuff that is at a very simple level, which helps me understand it. But it also helps the room understand where we're coming from. We break down the ambiguity. We break down the jargon. In government, jargon is king.

"You can always have an ISC and a VCS and a T3, 4 or 5. And that's got to make sure that that fits into the A772. And it's like where are we? What are we talking about? What's an A772? What's this? *What*? **So the facilitator can unscramble that language and help the process. Make people more visual; more thinking about what they've got to do"**

Be a Sneaky Vegetable: don't explain the theory, but involve people in the experience first.

Bob Dick says: "I don't try to explain what facilitation is. What I do instead is try to use experiential methods. I involve them in processes for building relationships, for instance, or for making decisions or planning, something like that. And then we step back from the experience that they have just had, and I ask them to tell me what worked there, what was it about the process that worked. So, what I am trying to do is not give them definitions but instead give them an experience of it, so they develop not just an intellectual understanding but one that is built into who they are. "

Social Intelligence is neither technical, nor process-focused. It's relational.

Bob Dick explains: "I think many people don't really think about how they do their conversation. They are on autopilot, doing it the way they have watched other people do it and the way they have learned. For me, Facilitation/Social Intelligence is about a whole range of alternative processes that allow people to be more engaged, to make better plans, to make better decisions, to do better at problem-solving."

Help people listen to each other's ideas.

Cheryl Gilroy says: "Be careful as a facilitator that you are not used as that conduit to define people's time and then the decision has already been made. The role of the Process Leader is to provide the mechanisms and the processes for people to listen to other people's ideas, to absolutely hear their concerns."

It's about creating a safe space for conversations.

Alan Halford says: "Primarily, in all my work, I create a safe environment for people to be able to say what they would like to say, to talk about the issues that they are passionate about with other people, and for other people to listen to them."

"Process leader role is to co-create a safe, purposeful, and responsive environment. Facilitation is what holds the environment as safe and purposeful"—Martin Ringer.

Martin Ringer continues: "The role of a Process Leader is to work with participants, to co-create a safe, purposeful, and responsive environment space. So, Facilitation/Social Intelligence is the providing of that container, environment, and climate, regardless of the contents of what the people are talking about. The Process Leaders are not coming in with opinions about the content of what people are talking about, but they provide the context, process, environment, and guidance to create that."

Process Leader supports everyone to do their best thinking.

Rhonda Tranks says: "Sam Kaine's statement was that the facilitator's role is to 'support everyone to do their best thinking.' Because, in meetings, we often have disasters, and people are not doing their best thinking, and they're not on their best behaviour, so they're not getting the best results. So, my role is to help them do that, and I describe myself as a Process Leader. I work not on 'what happens' in the meeting, but how it happens, so that they get their result. As I don't have a vested interest in the outcome, I help them work out what the outcome is that they want to get towards, and that's done collaboratively with people in the room."

The Process Leader stays outside of the content.

Richard Boyd says: "The Process Leader stays outside of the process in terms of the content and holds the space for people to have a safe framework, in which to bring their content, including their issues, emotions, and concerns. He or she has these concerns put out there systematically, or at least with some rigor or framework, without it all descending into chaos, so people have a common goal or mindset towards which they're heading."

Process Leader is a leadership role.

Andrew Rixon says: "A Process Leader is a leadership role. It's about being able to draw the answers from others and then work through and maintain the momentum."

Process Leader disrupts the existing habits and practices of the group.

Viv McWaters says: "My role I would describe as someone who is disrupting the existing habits and practices of the group. Typically, these groups come together and meet in a much-formalized structure. What I do is come in and disrupt that pattern.

"A lot of these agencies I've been working for are involved in working in communities that have been affected by natural disasters or have chronic, long-term issues such as drought and poverty. So the complexity and depth of the issues that they're dealing with can be overwhelming. It's important, as a Process Leader, to provide them that space where they can share their stories, their experiences, their successes, and their failures, and recognize that they bring their human elements to that. That they're not machines, and they're able to respond in a very human way to those very difficult issues.

"And when they have me working with them, basically what I'm doing is providing processes for them to interact and then getting out of the way and letting them get on with it."

Process Leader enables people to have ownership of an outcome.

Jules White says: "A well-facilitated workshop has ownership of all the people there. That's what the Process Leader does. It enables people to have ownership of an outcome that they want to achieve. They create a space, they observe what's going on, and they enable people to talk, see, achieve, and do what they have come to do."

Victor Konijn adds: "I think of myself as a process manager, making sure that the goal is clear at the beginning of every session as to why are we there together. Both on a goal level as well as on a practical level, I set how much time we need, what are we trying to achieve in that time, how we want to break it up. I need to understand what energy is in the room, where people are coming from, what they are feeling, and what they're experiencing.

"When they walk in, I need to identify what their expectations are and try to bring that to the surface, making sure it's all being heard, whether it's easy for people to be vocal or too vocal, or whether people don't feel like talking. We try to give the entire group an appreciation for who is in the room and what we can bring in, whatever the form."

Facilitation/Social Intelligence (SI) listens to people.

Cheryl Gilroy says: "Facilitation/Social Intelligence does this incredible thing. The incredible thing is that it listens to people. It allows a forum of people to be heard and to be taken seriously, and when people are taken seriously, magic occurs. I truly believe that everybody has genius in them, and it is really our job to find that, to tap into that and express it in a way that is really useful."

Social Intelligence is about providing the environment in which people can bring their ideas, their issues, and put them forward in a safe and supported way.

THE ROLE OF A PROCESS LEADER

***

Throughout this book, you will find more information from others and me about what the Process Leader does in the context of working with people in order to increase their group social intelligence.

In summary, here are the key points to remember:

- ✓ There is a distinct difference between a Process Leader, a trainer, a coach, an MC or a moderator, and that is their PURPOSE. A Process Leader also is neutral to the outcome of conversations and stays away from the content.
- ✓ It's about working with groups of people in a defined time and environment to help them achieve their goals, by increasing their group social intelligence.
- ✓ Process Leader role is mainly relational, not technical, although it requires some sneaky techniques to get people to talk to each other and help them make good decisions.

***

Read, reflect, and write down the key themes coming from the role of a Process Leader that you remember:

1. _____
   _____
   _____
   _____
   _____
   _____
   _____

2. _____
   _____
   _____
   _____
   _____
   _____
   _____

3. _____
   _____
   _____
   _____
   _____
   _____
   _____

CHAPTER 3

THE WORKPLACE FRAMEWORK

Like any other job, the role of a Process Leader also requires that a particular framework be in place in order to make the group do the work. The framework is formed by the quality of relationships between stakeholders, as well as the way principles are applied in a given environment. This environment is any confined space, often a workplace or anywhere the workshop takes place.

***

Why Would You Leave my Workshop?

I felt excited but fearful about one particular workshop. It was the biggest project this company had ever had to frame (meaning plan for), and I was asked to facilitate.

The main purpose of a framing-type workshop is to align stakeholders with the current and future situation and consider the phases of the project lifecycle. The final outcome is a roadmap, which is a plan that contains phases, gates, milestone dates, stakeholders involved, decision criteria, and the effort required.

This particular workshop involved a joint venture between two oil and gas giants, a category-1 megaproject in terms of the combination of high risk, high complexity, and high costs.

Preparation was key. I spent time with one of the project engineers to understand the context, complexities, and scope the plan, and then designed the workshop agenda. The agenda was signed, as were the confidentiality requirements.

The actual workshop started very well, with people turning up on time and gradually opening up to each other, so we could understand one another's roles and expectations.

Then something really unexpected happened later. After the grounding presentation was delivered, the project director stood up and announced that he needed to leave the room to fly out to Paris for joint venture (JV) negotiation, together with a third of the group members.

Why did only I seem shocked, at that time? Why had nobody told me anything beforehand?

I knew I had a plan prepared for the whole group and was totally motivated to apply the plan with no change. Five people leaving the workshop changed the whole dynamic of the room, however; especially because they were the people who *needed* to be there.

But I did not stop to check if people were actually ready for conversations about framing. I just continued. I wanted them to complete the frame more than they wanted to participate. When we got to define the future measures of success, people gave up participating.

"Without the leaders in the room, what chances do we have of actually making anything happen?" someone shouted.

I tried to persuade them to continue by telling them this is just a part of framing, which was needed anyway, but I soon realised I had no chance of winning with a group of people who just wanted to go home. They did leave shortly after, and I was left there by myself, feeling embarrassed and disappointed. I was upset for the group, for those leaders who left, and for myself.

"How dare you leave my workshop!" said the little voice in my head.

"The best way of learning from mistakes is to admit them, not blame them on someone else" (Anonymous)

This is what I learned from this and similar experiences:

- ✓ Have face-to-face meetings with your client directly at least once before the workshop. Your engagement with the client before the

workshop is as critical as your ability to engage with the group during the workshop
- ✓ Consider what people want at every stage of planning and conducting a workshop.
- ✓ Ideally, interview as many people as possible before the workshop
- ✓ Let people finish when they want to finish. Groups are not always ready to complete all the tasks that you want them to. Respect their state, wherever they are at.

The Workplace Relationship Triangle

Distinguish the **relationship triangle** that is between the Process Leader, the client (sponsor of the workshop), and the group of people participating in a workshop.

Simply:

The *Process Leader* is the person with the skills, knowledge, experience, and personal attributes to design and lead the processes in a workshop environment. He or she signs a contractual arrangement with the sponsor to make sure the objectives planned will be achieved. In addition, at the more informal level, the Process Leader is also responsible for the group: whatever happens in the group environment stays within this group and he or she supports the group to do their best thinking.

The *Client* or *Sponsor* of the workshop can be a leader or any other stakeholder who pays for the workshop and identifies the need for the Process

Leader to work with a group under agreed upon terms and conditions, including confidentiality agreements.

The *group of people* are members of a particular group that have a conscious or unconscious need to realise, and therefore they work with a Process Leader.

Typically, the Process Leader will receive an initial brief from the client, because a need for some group goals has been identified. Whether the Process Leader is an "internal" (a person whose role it is inside the organization to lead workshops) or an "external" (brought in from outside the organization), the client will describe their needs for the group development and the outcomes that they want to achieve, from an organizational point of view.

The Process Leader's role is to serve the group and ensure that the organisation and client outcomes are upheld and achieved through the group workshop interactions. Sometimes, these can be in conflict, and it is the Process Leader's skill that ensures the needs of all parties are taken into account.

Information Sharing

It is a necessary requirement of a successful workshop that the information shared between the Process Leader and the group remains confidential. This confidentiality is one of the primary reasons that the group feels comfortable entering into the Process Leader relationship. Confidentiality is also a key element in the association standards set by the International Organization of Facilitators' (IAF) *Ethics and Guidelines for Conduct* (see *Addendum 1*).

The Process Leader must agree, at the beginning of the assignment, what information is shared with the client and must have permission from the group to share the information. The information that is typically shared is an outcome from conversations.

One of the important roles in leading workshops is to help people find the confidence to communicate, to share information and to receive feedback willingly. If there is a conflict between the manager and the group, rather than the Process Leader being the "piggy in the middle," who is talking to both parties individually, both parties should be talking to each other! They all need to increase their social intelligence!

It's common for the Process Leader to be working with the group and then have periodic follow-up meetings with the client. These follow-up meetings are the opportunity to discuss the progress in group dynamics and the outcomes that the workshop has achieved, and to provide any other feedback about what the client would like to see, moving forward. Let the client give feedback to the Process Leader, rather than the other way around.

On the topic of feedback to the client, I once asked my client, "Have you given the group this feedback already? What was their response?"

My client said, "Yes, I've given them the feedback, but they just don't seem to be listening or taking it on.

I encouraged the client to be a part of the next workshop and play a role where he could fully express what was important and why. Then the group would have a chance to be open in their communication about what mattered to them. This would foster more open dialogue and a culture where people listened to each other.

What Does the Framework Look Like?

The Social Intelligence Framework is based on the principle that the Process Leader has a number of credentials, ethics, competencies, and tools that are demonstrated, applied, and focused on, in order to help a group achieve better outcomes.

Each of the segments represents what the Process Leader brings to the relationship triangle, along with their personal attributes of passion, energy, and commitment.

These segments can be best thought of as a horizontal hierarchy that supports the group.

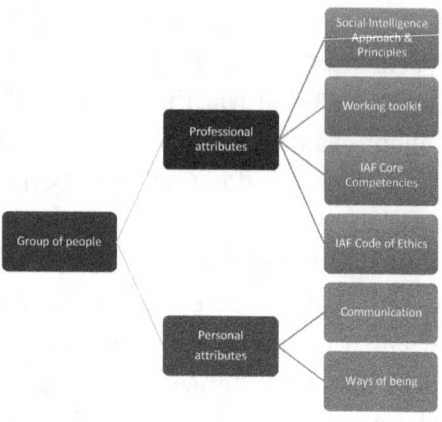

Refer to the IAF Code of Conduct as well as IAF Core Competencies established by the International Organisation of Facilitators, with details in my Addendums 1 and 2 at the back of the book.

Communication, which includes listening and speaking up, is of a particular nature. Listening is more about seeking to understand where the participants are coming from; speaking up is more about the ability to nurture the group, provoke, help them to reflect and enquire in such a way that they begin to understand one another's contributions and involvement, rather than emphasize their differences.

I will expand on developing the skillset of a Process Leader in Book 2, which is dedicated to growth, learning, and performance.

Social Intelligence Principles

So, what are some of the things, conditions, or let's call them **critical success factors** that need to be in place in order to get the most out of this work?

***

Initially, I had in mind some of the obvious things like:

- ✓ A plan for a workshop
- ✓ People involved
- ✓ Understanding of the context
- ✓ Logistics, including preparing the papers and toolbox you need.

These are some of the obvious necessities, and it's highly likely you already know them. But what else?

What is specific to a facilitated workshop that we need to establish that will have a direct impact on its success?

Brainstorm some of the aspects of those questions:

What makes a Process Leader do a good job?

_____

_____

_____

_____

_____

_____

_____

_____

Safety for truth-speaking

Nick Preston: "Create a psychologically safe environment for people to speak their truth and design processes where that truth speaking actually influences decisions. That is how I would describe it."

Creating a safe environment for truth-speaking.

"The first desire of every human being is to be taken seriously. So, as a Process Leader, you need to create an environment where every idea and every point of view is taken seriously. An environment where everyone gets heard.

"When people experience being genuinely heard half of the conflict dies away, because the first desire is to be taken seriously. When you dismiss, belittle, talk over, talk down, ignore, or debate a person's point of view without exhausting the desire to see and to understand it is impossible for a Process Leader to actually embody the very principles that they want a group to embody.

"This is the idea of *imitation*, which means a Process Leader has to create certain kinds of open behaviours worthy of imitation by their group. Honesty and truth-speaking starts with the Process

Leader first, and that trust is then transferred to the sponsor, to the people in the room, and then to the wider community. That is how it works," Neil says.

Truth-speaking reduces risk

"That is it. It is that simple. The biggest mistakes and errors that are made in infrastructure, whatever they might be, come from a pervasive culture that works in the shadow of the organisation. It basically says to the people in the room, "Don't tell us what we need to know." So, if you have a culture where decisions have already been made before the facilitated process occurs, then often the organisation makes incredibly naïve assumptions, both about the nature of the problem and the solution. Social Intelligence work is used as a kind of feel-good exercise.

"One shouldn't use a Process Leader in an organisation unless the organisation is genuinely interested in people solving their problems. If they are not interested, there is a good chance that they only partially know the nature of the problem and its solution, thus increasing the risk profile of the organisation.

"So, truth-speaking is essential to reduce risk," says Neil Preston.

Collaborative Learning

Belinda Coghlan says: "Well, I think facilitation allows all people to hear and be heard, allows the collective wisdom of the group, and allows for collective learning."

Surfacing the collective

"When there is change, there is conflict. The wisdom of the group is much more than the wisdom of the individual, and we share our life experiences. We don't actually teach people anything. We use a system of what we call 'co-learning' or 'collaborative learning.' That is the way we work," says Alan Halford.

"It is about learning from each other and fitting all those little jigsaw pieces together to create a picture. It is all about taking away the authority and power that people have and allowing people to collectively problem-solve without that ranking dynamic. It addresses not only the power and balance but also people who dominate, people who are and aren't quiet."

"So, establishing Social Intelligence at any workplace really enables *all* people to hear and be heard."

Process versus Content

"There is a fundamental distinction between the *process* and the *content*. It is crucial that the Process Leader and the client are aware about that difference.

"The *content* is the substance of the conversation. You want to invite people to the workshop who have a particular stake in the substance, either directly or because they have an impact -or an influence on that substance.

"Knowledge of a particular topic or substance generates an opinion about it and judgment towards other people's opinions. That is why it is very hard to facilitate conversations if you have a particular opinion or stand on a given subject."–Bob Dick.

Jules White says, "When I'm a Process Leader, I'm there to do a role. I'm not there to be the expert. For me, the people who are there are the experts on the content. They may or may not have a university degree as the experts, but they're the people there, they're the ones that have to make the decisions. They're the ones that have to come up with solutions. So, for me, they are the experts.

Whenever I work and walk into the room, I just hold the space for them to have that conversation about the content that they've chosen to talk about."

Finding Common Ground

Amrit Kendrick says: "I am called a 'classroom leader.' So I work with a group of individuals who come from all walks of life—I have teachers, musicians, artists, business people—and they are working as a group, over time.

"One of the most powerful things for them is to declare that they have a certain set of goals, as a group and as individuals. And then, periodically, maybe once a week, once a month, once every three months, they stop and have a conversation as a group, which we call a 'conversation for completion.' These completion conversations allow the group to clear away anything that has been harboured or held onto during this process.

"What happens in human groups, when they work together, is often they declare big visions and plan great goals, and then they head off in that direction. The typical human scenario is that one person doesn't do what they said they were going to do, and another person makes them wrong and complains or doesn't even complain, just holds it against them and stops trusting them. Then, someone else gets stopped from doing what they promised, because someone else didn't do what they promised, and they use that as a justification to not do what they said. It gets very, very messy in groups.

"This completion process allows people to stop and actually get honest with each other and truthfully state how they have been operating and then forgive each other, forgive themselves, and get back to a place where they can re-declare themselves as teammates, as people who are working towards the same goal and then keep going again.

"Finding common ground is one of the really important elements of facilitated workshops."

Do the best you can with them

Joy Humphreys says: "I think there's something important about how you conduct yourself, but also what your own philosophy is. I love people. I think that, if I can be generous, that's the least I can do, because it's about paying it forward. If I can do the best I can with other people, then that's what I can do. 'Do no harm'. And I also have a principle, 'Do the best you can with them,' which translates into:

- ❖ Believe in them
- ❖ Be present with them
- ❖ Be present with yourself
- ❖ Be OK to work with unknown in an uncertain space
- ❖ Be strong in that space
- ❖ Have no control
- ❖ Go with the flow
- ❖ Work emergently.

"I think that I'm absolutely privileged. I'm the luckiest girl alive to have the work that I have. I really am. I love it. I'm so, so lucky to do what I do."

Janet Rice adds: "There's a lot of really taking the needs of the group into account and helping the group to reach the outcomes that they want to reach, whether it's a decision or discussion about how they feel about something. Most of the work that I do is strategic planning workshops, where it's a group or an organisation that wants to work out what their aims are over the next period of time. So you're helping them with appropriate processes to work through all the issues involved and helping them to create a clear direction ahead out of what can seem like a real jumble of information and a huge amount of complexity, and then creating order out of that complexity."

Working Toolkit

Every Process Leader needs a foundation toolkit to operate in their group environment.

For me, it is the opportunity framing process. Most of my work is about helping project groups define the frame for their venture, whether it is a business venture, an initiative, a new idea, or new ways of working. The process is based on understanding that, whatever you do, you can divide it into some phases, and there is always a decision point to proceed or not to the next phase. In order to make this decision, a plan needs to be defined and the work completed needs to be of a desired quality.

I use several different tools that aim at helping groups to understand the current situation, define the future they want, and then creating the "bridging" tools that help to bridge the gap between the current and future situations.

Framing-type workshops are very powerful and engaging. They are especially beneficial for teams with a high level of diversity in terms of skills, knowledge, experience, and expectations. They bring a lot of clarity about what needs to be done, who with, and how, by addressing the following key items:

- Typical issues, questions and concerns
- Risks from uncertainties
- Decisions and facts already made from decisions we need to focus on now
- Value drivers from enablers and other reasons
- What does success look like from the next milestone achieved?
- Who do we need to engage with now and who needs to be kept informed only?

This toolkit helps me to design other types of workshops, including strategic planning, stakeholders' engagement, visioning, and team alignment, even team-building events.

I will share more about the development of a Process Leader, including examples from others, in the second book in this series.

Here are some key points to remember:

- ✓ Commit to engage with both the client and the group of people you work with
- ✓ Familiarise yourself with IAF Code of conduct and Core competencies (see addendums) at the back of the book
- ✓ There are some distinct principles to demonstrate in every workshop, including safety for truth-speaking, process versus the content, and creating common ground
- ✓ Develop a basic toolkit to operate from.

CHAPTER 4

THE BENEFITS ACHIEVED

I couldn't believe what I saw initially. Before a whole-day workshop had finished, the team had found a problem resolution and consensus on the way forward! Those blokes who couldn't even talk to each other were now expressing gratitude and thanks for contributions and listening. My head was spinning.

Facilitation when applied properly can cure any group of people.

I have worked with a number of clients from various organizations, as well as with some non-profits, on how to engage with each other in ways that help to align their goals with their expectations. What has become clear to me is that most people, no matter what their position in the organisation, want to be heard and want to hear others.

Facilitation Helps People Hear Each Other

Each time I work with any group of people, I find that:

❖ Facilitated workshops help to achieve healthier results with less time

❖ Members of those groups get to know themselves better, which improves their ways of working and communication, and increases group social intelligence

❖ Designing workshop structure is as important as preparing yourself to lead the group.

❖ Focus is changing from "my wellness" to "our wellness."

Knowing how to heal ourselves is not enough. We need to have the same healthy approach to group work and team management.

Let's face it: each of us is part of some sort of group, whether it be at work, at home with our families, or in any social context. We are all challenged by the way we do things together, our thinking, the way we listen to each other, and how we speak, and—plan, as we have all had different experiences; and all come from different cultural perspectives.

Facilitated workshops offer new ways for approaching old problems, especially when you feel you are stuck and want to make some progress.

Chantal Harris adds: "As a Process Leader, you can start to see how organisations have their own cultures. It enables separate groups to start to get to know each other more and learn a bit more about each other. You may have a community that has a really good proposal, but the business they are working with has constantly said no to the proposal, or isn't engaging with the community.

"In something like a facilitation, you get to sit down and find out exactly what the community wants to do, how they want to do it, and why they want to do it, and then be able to turn that into the correct kind of language, and maybe the right process.

"Maybe there are some checks and balances or due diligence or something that needs to happen from the company side of things, so that the groups actually move closer together. Then the company can start to understand why it is that the community is so passionate about something.

"The benefit is to have people from two really different spaces actually start to blend into a third space together that says, 'Okay, as a business, we can now understand where the community is coming from,' and see some of the things that it would benefit from by having this project up and running. Then the community also understands that, from a business perspective, there are some things commercially or maybe legally or whatever it may be that need to get signed off first, and then they can move forward together on the same page. So, for me, that is a definite benefit: to watch people come from their own space and start to create a space together where they can understand each other better and move towards that common goal."

Chantal Harris continues, "The biggest value for businesses, whenever they engage in genuine group dynamic, is learning and understanding what is best and the opportunity to hear from the people themselves. There are some incredible individuals in these communities who can really help the process and benefit the organisations by being part of that process. It can save companies a lot of time and resources down the track by having that facilitation done early on in programs and processes."

Claire Vanderplank says, "The benefit that they get is not always the benefit that they think they are getting.

"A great analogy is this; when I was doing facilitation training, I always used to tell this to the group. It is kind of like having this massive, big, fat elephant in the middle of the room, and everyone sitting around it, but you can't tell the nature of the beast from any one particular point where you are sitting. I mean from one side, there might be a massive big pink spot that I wouldn't know was there, because I am on the other side. So you really do have to hear from everyone in order to see exactly what it is you are dealing with.

The benefit of involving diverse perspectives is yes, it makes it harder to come to a consensus, but you don't miss stuff that you really should have known, so you get much more appropriate and innovative problem solving."

Solving wicked or complex problems

Neil Preston says: "As a psychologist, **intention is everything**. The key is to discern the intention of the client.

"Clients can often say, 'We want you to get an outcome we have already determined, and so we want you to facilitate that outcome.' I don't tend to enjoy working in that space and tend to move away from it. My clients and colleagues use what we call an 'emergent design practice,' and that is that the solutions literally emerge out of the facilitated environment or what we call 'safe holding environments' for truth to be spoken.

"The reason is that if the problem is complex, no one actually has a monopoly on the solution, and so, if a client has a genuinely wicked problem, a problem that requires the complex wisdom of a crowd, then we would do a lot of coaching about the use of those kinds of technologies to solve that problem. What you end up doing is coaching the sponsor or the client about learning to let go of their own need to actually control the situation. So, the facilitated approach that we use is a lot more emergent, and, in fact, the more wicked or complex the problem, the more emergent the technologies that we use. Only clients we have worked with over a number of years that have really high collaborative maturity are able to use those technologies to their greatest benefit, because they know that it works. So, intention is everything.

"If a client genuinely doesn't know the answer to a problem because it is too complex, then I am your man, because emergent practice or emergent design (and what we mean by 'emergent design' is any form of design—that could be a process, an organisational structure, a change-management initiative, whatever design that emerges from the wisdom of the crowd—comes out of that safe psychological environment) always works. And the reason why it works is because the psychological literature shows that collective intelligence is an emergent property that is always higher than the sums of individual intelligences. What I mean by that is if you get a whole bunch of smart experts together around a problem, it is not as accurate or as elegant a solution as the collective wisdom of a group of people. I hope that makes sense.

"If it is complex, collaborate, because collaboration is commensurate to complexity. If you have a complex problem, you have to collaborate with other people, not because it is nice, but because it is needed, as the nature of the problem is complex. You can't solve it alone.

"If it is complicated, like putting a man on the moon—believe it or not, that is complicated, but not complex—then you can use experts. But if it is complex, like, say, climate change, you need a whole mob in the room. So the benefits of facilitation are that 'we are better together.'

"All the research shows, as well, that if you get a group of people working collaboratively (not cooperatively, compliantly, or coercively; I'm talking about a genuinely collaborative group), the solutions tend to be more elegant. And what makes them more elegant is the level of shared commitment and understanding around the nature of both the problem and its solution.

"So there is another 'Neil-ism' that you can take from this, and that is: 'When meaning triumphs over motivation, the change comes for free.' So we are making sense of the world. When it makes sense, people move, and the best way to do that is through dialogue. And one way to do that is by using process leaders. That is why I do it."

Making better decisions

Janet Rice says: "It's basically empowerment, and it's helping them to build their own community. It's about realising the power of people working together and what one can achieve. I think that the facilitation processes have helped them to have a very constructive experience of how people in groups can work together to achieve change. They come to realise that you can work together, that you can sort out what you want to do and then take that out into the world, encouraging other people to work together and working with them. I think the group skills that they have gained through the course will help them as community leaders to be able to work with other people throughout the rest of their lives, basically, and continue to build on those processes.

"You get better decisions, and you also have much more productive and harmonious outcomes. You're not wasting time just fighting each other all the time. You avoid the whole adversarial process, where people, instead of working productively together, are actually achieving good outcomes. It's really by investing in those good processes that you can have something where you get, you know, it might not be the number one preference of either the developer or the government or the community, but it's something that everyone can live with, so we can just get on and implement it.

"And you really do have a sense of people having involvement in decisions that affect their lives, so people can have genuinely a much better constructive engagement with their government, which means that there's a sense of value in engagement with their government. So, you get that community participation in government and government processes, as well. At the moment, in Australian society, we have people who feel totally disengaged. They feel they're not being listened to.

They feel there's no point in being involved, there's no point in voting even, because what's the point of voting if you're only going to elect a politician who's not going to listen to me?"

Janet Rice continues, "And so, if we really want to, we have got lots of challenges that our communities are facing in the world, and in order to tackle them, we need to be involving people from all walks of life and in everything that's happening, in order to get change. So, by having processes that people can genuinely be involved in and feel, "I was a part of that" and "I was really listened to," and the outcome has taken "my views" into account, this all really builds that sense of community and builds engagement in our democratic processes."

Equal involvement

John Dawson says, "Well, one thing is that Process Leaders enable everyone to be equally involved. For participants in any organisation, it enables them to take part in the workshop and whatever is created in the workshop (outcome). That's one thing.

"For managers applying Social Intelligence techniques themselves, they may get bogged down with their issues and their operational daily stuff but by having a Process Leader there who keeps them on track and to the purpose that they expect, they will actually achieve what they want to get out of the day and probably a lot more, as well. And they learn a few things about one another on the way. Also, the Process Leader can push and challenge them. These challenges can challenge their ways of working, which they probably wouldn't do as much themselves, because they're used to working with one another, and I guess the personality and ego and relationship thing gets in the way a bit."

Neil Preston adds: "Shared commitment through shared understanding—that is the mantra. That is what we are there to get: commitment towards a solution that has the greatest rationale with the greatest number of people in the room.

"My work essentially as a psychologist, particularly as an organisational psychologist, is to move from the interpersonal psychology to transpersonal psychology. And western people are hopelessly equipped for transpersonal psychology; there is too much emphasis on 'me' and 'my,' rather than the transpersonal, which is 'us' and 'ours.'

"So the kind of dialogical approach to solving problems requires quite mature relationships to both the nature of the problem and ambiguity. That is, if it is complex and you have a whole range of different views in the room, it is going to be ambiguous. Managers will close down a problem as quickly as they can and claim it is solved, and leaders will lean into the ambiguity as opportunity. That is what I have noticed as the difference between managers and leaders in highly complex areas. It is their level and degree to which they can handle ambiguity.

"The more complex a problem is, the more ambiguous it is, so a lot of the work I am doing is actually coaching both individuals and teams to deal with ambiguity and emergence, to handle that the idea that comes out of the facilitated process is, by and large, greater than the idea that you came with into the facilitation" –Neil Preston.

Rick Sommerford says, "I think the biggest advantage or the greatest good that has come of it all is that I have been able to generate trust and association or community within my work group. That is, people are prepared to stand up for what they believe in, which is always good, but they are also prepared to listen to the reasoning of others.

"This is a process over time, I guess. I think that you can create a situation where people generate trust amongst themselves. Not just that you bring that trust, but they generate it themselves when you give them the opportunities. So, to bring communities or the community opinion to the attention of business and to likewise bring the goals and aspirations of a business into the community's mind is an extremely valuable tool, and I think that facilitators are uniquely positioned to provide that 'lubricant,' if you like, between the social and business sectors.

"Business and communities are often at odds, as many people would understand. Business has a particular goal, and most of that is wrapped around profit, although a lot of businesses these days are starting to understand that profit is not the only goal. There are a lot of businesses, and, in particular, the business that I am most familiar with in recent years, the oil and gas exploration business, seeks to be acceptable within their community. I think that is a change. And it has been articulated by facilitators much like yourself, Iwona, where you act on behalf of a business, but you have the awareness of how important it is for the community to have trust within that business operation."

Rob Carolane adds: "People being able to understand their role and make their decisions about direction. It is not always possible to deliver that, but that is my intent. To be able to deliver that."

Viv McWaters says, "I think some of the benefits would be they get a visceral experience. So, instead of just bringing their head to a workshop and intellectualizing how they might respond or what they might do, they actually have a physical, visceral experience to what that might be like.

"Some of the processes that I use involve people improvising different approaches to different scenarios. They feel what that's like, and they feel what works, rather than trying to intellectualize what might work.

"And, for example, if somebody from the audience says, 'Why doesn't Billy try this?' I usually say, 'Let's not hear a suggestion. Let's get you up to show us what that looks like.' So, people get a far more involved experience in my workshops, and they also move around quite a lot. It's a lot of physical activity, because I think that, especially in Southeast Asia and Africa, there's been a lot of emphasis on the invited expert and listening to what *they* say and writing down what *they* say.

"And that's a very traditional model of transferring knowledge and information. It doesn't necessarily tap into the knowledge and wisdom that is in the group, which is what my workshops try and do."

Facilitating your own growth

Martin Ringer says: "What struck me from very early on from, working with adolescents and really hard, tough-love criminals or whatever, was, when the conditions were right, how strong the urges were in every human being to be human. There is an incredible growth period in most people, but it can take some leading to any change.

"Frequent exposure to facilitation in a pressured environment drives people to grow, to connect with other people, and to connect with purpose. Growth in a well-engineered space can be remarkable, because facilitation is a good process that involves the release of a lot of unconscious pressures.

"The facilitator and the facilitated are part of the same system, so when remarkable things are happening with the participants, this also spins off to the facilitators. So I've experienced a great deal of learning, growth, and excitement. Also, obviously, great times of pain and frustration. But, overall, being a facilitator has facilitated my own growth. Groups quite often provide surprises. The facilitator can be very well prepared, have the program all organised, and know exactly what type of exercises and what type of outcomes they want, and then something unusual will happen, something they weren't expecting.-"So the really brilliant facilitator is the one who can think on their feet and still cause the outcomes, regardless of any breakdowns or unforeseen reactions or expressions that come out." —Martin Ringer.

Rick Sommerford says, "I guess the biggest thing that I have learned about myself is not to impose my views on anyone and, in particular, the views that I have held over a very long time. It has almost become a law unto me, to not impose those views on anybody else but to seek other people's views on those things. In fact, what happens and what has happened for me, is that I have moderated my own views over time and have become much more accepting of others."

***

Here are some key points to remember about facilitated workshops:

- ✓ Improve team communication
- ✓ Promote collaboration and help in reaching commitment
- ✓ Result in team-based solutions.

Before you move on to the next book, reflect and write down your own answers to the following questions:

1. What benefit could you get for yourself and your team from participating in facilitated workshops?

_____

_____

_____

_____

_____

_____

_____

_____

_____

_____

_____

2. Who do you need to be and what you need to develop in yourself to become a Process Leader?

_____

_____

_____

_____

_____

_____

_____

_____

_____

_____

_____

Read, reflect, get inspired, and connect...

###

ADDENDUM 1:

Statement of Value and Code of Ethics

(Source: The International Organisation of Facilitators (IAF))

Statement of Values

As group facilitators, we believe in the inherent value of the individual and the collective wisdom of the group. We strive to help the group make the best use of the contributions of each of its members. We set aside our personal opinions and support the group's right to make its own choices. We believe that collaborative and cooperative interaction builds consensus and produces meaningful outcomes. We value professional collaboration to improve our profession.

Code of Ethics

1. Client Service

We are in service to our clients, using our group facilitation competencies to add value to their work.

Our clients include the groups we facilitate and those who contract with us on their behalf. We work closely with our clients to understand their expectations so that we provide the appropriate service, and that the group produces the desired outcomes. It is our responsibility to ensure that we are competent to handle the intervention. If the group decides it needs to go in a direction other than that originally intended by either the group or its representatives, our role is to help the group move forward, reconciling the original intent with the emergent direction.

2. Conflict of Interest

We openly acknowledge any potential conflict of interest.

Prior to agreeing to work with our clients, we discuss openly and honestly any possible conflict of interest, personal bias, prior knowledge of the organisation or any other matter which may be perceived as preventing us from working effectively with the interests of all group members. We do this so that, together, we may make an informed decision about proceeding and to prevent misunderstanding that could detract from the success or credibility of the clients or ourselves. We refrain from using our position to secure unfair or inappropriate privilege, gain, or benefit.

3. Group Autonomy

We respect the culture, rights, and autonomy of the group.

We seek the group's conscious agreement to the process and their commitment to participate. We do not impose anything that risks the welfare and dignity of the participants, the freedom of choice of the group, or the credibility of its work.

4. Processes, Methods, and Tools

We use processes, methods and tools responsibly.

In dialogue with the group or its representatives we design processes that will achieve the group's goals, and select and adapt the most appropriate methods and tools. We avoid using processes, methods or tools with which we are insufficiently skilled, or which are poorly matched to the needs of the group.

5. Respect, Safety, Equity, and Trust

We strive to engender an environment of respect and safety where all participants trust that they can speak freely and where individual boundaries are honoured. We use

our skills, knowledge, tools, and wisdom to elicit and honour the perspectives of all.

We seek to have all relevant stakeholders represented and involved. We promote equitable relationships among the participants and facilitator and ensure that all participants have an opportunity to examine and share their thoughts and feelings. We use a variety of methods to enable the group to access the natural gifts, talents and life experiences of each member. We work in ways that honour the wholeness and self-expression of others, designing sessions that respect different styles of interaction. We understand that any action we take is an intervention that may affect the process.

6. Stewardship of Process

We practice stewardship of process and impartiality toward content.

While participants bring knowledge and expertise concerning the substance of their situation, we bring knowledge and expertise concerning the group interaction process. We are vigilant to minimize our influence on group outcomes. When we have content knowledge not otherwise available to the group, and that the group must have to be effective, we offer it after explaining our change in role.

7. Confidentiality

We maintain confidentiality of information.

We observe confidentiality of all client information. Therefore, we do not share information about a client within or outside of the client's organisation, nor do we report on group content, or the individual opinions or behaviour of members of the group without consent.

8. Professional Development

We are responsible for continuous improvement of our facilitation skills and knowledge.

We continuously learn and grow. We seek opportunities to improve our knowledge and facilitation skills to better assist groups in their work. We remain current in the field of facilitation through our practical group experiences and ongoing personal development. We offer our skills within a spirit of collaboration to develop our professional work practices.

***

The Core Facilitator Competencies framework was developed over several years by the IAF with the support of its members and facilitators from all over the world. Tested over time, the six competencies form the basic set of skills, knowledge, and behaviours that facilitators must have in order to be successful facilitating in a wide variety of environments.

ADDENDUM 2:

The Core Competencies

(Source: The International Association of Facilitators (IAF))

A. CREATE COLLABORATIVE CLIENT RELATIONSHIPS

A1) Develop working partnerships

Clarify mutual commitment

Develop consensus on tasks, deliverables, roles & responsibilities

Demonstrate collaborative values and processes such as in co-facilitation

A2) Design and customise applications to meet client needs

Analyse organisational environment

Diagnose client need

Create appropriate designs to achieve intended outcomes

Predefine a quality product & outcomes with client

A3) Manage multi-session events effectively

Contract with client for scope and deliverables

Develop event plan

Deliver event successfully

Assess / evaluate client satisfaction at all stages of the event or project

B. PLAN APPROPRIATE GROUP PROCESSES

B1) Select clear methods and processes that:

Foster open participation with respect for client culture, norms and participant diversity

Engage the participation of those with varied learning or thinking styles

Achieve a high quality product or outcome that meets the client needs

B2) Prepare time and space to support group process

Arrange physical space to support the purpose of the meeting

Plan effective use of time

Provide effective atmosphere and drama for sessions

C. CREATE AND SUSTAIN A PARTICIPATORY ENVIRONMENT

C1) Demonstrate effective participatory and interpersonal communication skills

Apply a variety of participatory processes

Demonstrate effective verbal communication skills

Develop rapport with participants

Practice active listening

Demonstrate ability to observe and provide feedback to participants

C2) Honour and recognise diversity, ensuring inclusiveness

Encourage positive regard for the experience and perception of all participants

Create a climate of safety and trust

Create opportunities for participants to benefit from the diversity of the group

Cultivate cultural awareness and sensitivity

C3) Manage group conflict

Help individuals identify and review underlying assumptions

Recognise conflict and its role within group learning / maturity

Provide a safe environment for conflict to surface

Manage disruptive group behaviour

Support the group through resolution of conflict

C4) Evoke group creativity

Draw out participants of all learning/thinking styles

Encourage creative thinking

Accept all ideas

Use approaches that best fit needs and abilities of the group

Stimulate and tap group energy

D. GUIDE GROUP TO APPROPRIATE AND USEFUL OUTCOMES

D1) Guide the group with clear methods and processes

Establish clear context for the session

Actively listen, question and summarise to elicit the sense of the group

Recognise tangents and redirect to the task

Manage small and large group process

D2) Facilitate group self-awareness about its task

Vary the pace of activities according to needs of group

Identify information the group needs, and draw out data and insight from the group

Help the group synthesise patterns, trends, root causes, frameworks for action

Assist the group in reflection on its experience

D3) Guide the group to consensus and desired outcomes

Use a variety of approaches to achieve group consensus

Use a variety of approaches to meet group objectives

Adapt processes to changing situations and needs of the group

Assess and communicate group progress

Foster task completion

E. BUILD AND MAINTAIN PROFESSIONAL KNOWLEDGE

E1) Maintain a base of knowledge

Be knowledgeable in management, organisational systems and development, group development, psychology, and conflict resolution

Understand dynamics of change

Understand learning/ thinking theory

E2) Know a range of facilitation methods

Understand problem solving and decision-making models

Understand a variety of group methods and techniques

Know consequences of misuse of group methods

Distinguish process from task and content

Learn new processes, methods, & models in support of client's changing/emerging needs

E3) Maintain professional standing

Engage in ongoing study / learning related to our field

Continuously gain awareness of new information in our profession

Practice reflection and learning

Build personal industry knowledge and networks

Maintain certification

F. MODEL POSITIVE PROFESSIONAL ATTITUDE

F1) Practice self-assessment and self-awareness

Reflect on behaviour and results

Maintain congruence between actions and personal and professional values

Modify personal behaviour / style to reflect the needs of the group

Cultivate understanding of one's own values and their potential impact on work with clients

F2) Act with integrity

Demonstrate a belief in the group and its possibilities

Approach situations with authenticity and a positive attitude

Describe situations as facilitator sees them and inquire into different views

Model professional boundaries and ethics (as described in the IAF's **Statement of Values and Code of Ethics)**

F3) Trust group potential and model neutrality

Honour the wisdom of the group

Encourage trust in the capacity and experience of others

Vigilant to minimise influence on group outcomes

Maintain an objective, non-defensive, non-judgmental stance.

ADDENDUM 3:

Contributors' Profiles

We would like to say a big thank you again to the amazing Process Leaders who have contributed heaps to make this book possible. Many of them have their own books and other educational products. For more information, feel free to contact them directly.

Alan Halford
The Conflict Company
Phone: +61 (0) 421 475 252
Email: alan@conflictcompany.com.au
www.conflictcompany.com.au
Perth, Australia

Amrit Kendrick
Sustain Nature Communication
Phone: +61 (0) 400 628 830
Email: amrit@westnet.com.au
Perth, Australia

Andrew Rixon
Babel Fish Group
Phone: +61 (0) 400 352 809
Email: andrew@babelfishgroup.com
www.babelfishgroup.com
Melbourne, Australia

Belinda Coghlan
OD Consulting Services
Phone: +61 (0) 414 642921
Email: belindacoghlan@iprimus.com.au
www.odconsultingservices.com.au
Perth, Australia

Bob Dick
Founder of AFN
(Australian Asian Facilitators Network)
Phone: +61 7 3378 5365
Email: bd@bigpond.net.au
www.aral.com.au
Brisbane, Australia

Chantal Harris
The Cultural Connection Code
Phone: +61 (0) 448 022 603
Email: chantal@theculturalconnectioncode.com
www.theculturalconnectioncode.com
Perth, Australia

Claire Vanderplank
Phone: +61 (0) 431980094
Email: womcreation@gmail.com
www.weaponsofmasscreation.com.au
Perth, Australia

Cheryl Gilroy
People Dynamics
Phone: +61 (0) 413009290
Email: gilroy@peopledynamics.com.au
www.peopledynamics.com.au
Brisbane, Australia

Cindy Tonkin
Phone: +61 (0) 412 135 426
Email: cindy@cindytonkin.com
www.cindytonkin.com
Sydney, Australia

Janet Rice
Phone: +61 (0) 400 352 935
Email: senator.rice@aph.gov.au
http://janetrice.com.au
Melbourne, Australia

Jeremy Lu, GroupMap
Phone: +61(0) 416 155 175
Email: info@groupmap.com
www.groupmap.com
Perth, Australia

Jill Chivers
Phone: +61 (0) 416 074 911
Email: jill@jillchivers.com
www.jillchivers.com
Queensland, Australia

John Dawson
Phone: +64 219 99 833
Email: john@4thway.co.nz
www.4thway.co.nz
Auckland, New Zealand

Jules White
Phone: +61 (0) 419 303 856
Email: circlesoftruth@wetnet.com.au
Melbourne, Australia

Joy Humphreys
The Humphreys Group
Phone: +61 (0) 412 128 565
Email: joy@humphreysgroup.com.au
www.humphreysgroup.com.au
Melbourne, Australia

Martin Ringer
Group Institute International
Phone: +61 431 421 834
Email: martinringer@groupinstitute.com
www.groupinstitute.com
Perth, Australia

Neil Preston
PsyOpus Pty Ltd
Phone: +61 (0) 439 946 869
Email: neilpreston@psyopus.com.au
www: psyopus.com.au
Perth, Australia

Nick Housego, CPF
Phone: +61 (0) 414 59 82 97
Email: nousego@gmail.com
Canberra, Australia

Rick Sommerford
Email: taichoda1@yahoo.com.au
Perth, Australia

Rhonda Tranks, CPF
Illuma Consulting
Phone: +61 (0) 410 510 720
Email: info@illumaconsulting.com.au
www.illumaconsulting.com.au
Melbourne, Australia

Richard Boyd
Energetics Institute
Conscious Business Australia
Phone: +61 (0) 414 897 024
Email: info@energeticsinstitute.com.au
www.energeticsinstitute.com.au
Perth, Australia

Rob Carolane
Twin Prism
Phone: +61 (0) 409 870 932
Email: rob@twinprism.com.au
www.twinprism.com.au
Victoria, Australia

Viv McWaters
Beyond the Edge Pty Ltd.
Phone: +61 (0) 417 135 406
Email: info@vivmcwaters.com.au
www.vivmcwaters.com.au
Victoria, Australia

Victor Konijn
Clarity Counts
Office: +61 2 9401 5516
Mobile: +61 404 067 640
Email: victor@claritycounts.com.au
www.claritycounts.com.au
Sydney, Australia

#

SPECIAL THANKS

Special thanks to the wonderful minds who helped as interviewers, contributors, transcribers, translators, editors, proofreaders, friends, and supporters, including those who helped me in my journey by helping to broaden my skillset, show me opportunities, provide me with feedback and support, and cause me to be so passionate about facilitation.

Big thanks to Karl Nolte, Susanna Durston, David Newman, Michael Morison, Bob Dick, Andrew Jobling, Pam Brossman, Ingrid Gipson and especially Kathryn Galán and Maree Wrack for their great advice and help with editing and proofreading.

I acknowledge especially the people whom I interviewed. I appreciate their honesty when they shared about themselves and the work they have already done. They are stellar examples of facilitation as a profession. I look up to them with admiration. These are people who started out exactly like you and me: with a dream to pursue organizational success and life happiness.

Big thanks to my mum, dad, and my brother who have always believed in me and supported me on my journey the best they could, even though they can hardly understand what I do as a Process Leader or quality assurance specialist.

Finally, special thanks to my partner Austin Wilson, the most amazing man I've ever met, an "organic" facilitator who helped me to sculpt this series of books, and without whom I would not have the courage and determination to continue doing what I love to do.

Not to forget caffeine and chocolate, my companions through many a long night of writing.

BOOK 1: WHAT IS FACILITATION?

ABOUT THE AUTHORS

IWONA POLOWY

Iwona was born in Poland and raised by parents who were small business owners during the time when her country was transitioning from communism to democracy. She soon learned that all people want social calm, and that everyone seeks participation and clarity in decision-making.

Iwona's people skills were apparent from an early age, but the spirit of making things happen lit up in her much later, when she moved to Wroclaw to study engineering and economics. She then became an active participant in various students clubs, including "Wigor" and her own student's organisation, the Total Quality Management Group.

This led her to move to London a year before Poland joined the European Union, in June 2003, to learn English and to pursue life happiness. During her first year in London, she worked hard, studying the language and reading countless books, while doing several part time jobs to pay her bills. She advanced her social skills by taking on many volunteer jobs and observing what makes people tick.

Her first professional job was in London with the Institute of Quality Assurance, coordinating training and educational courses. Then she joined the oil and gas industry, moving quickly up the career ladder, from Quality Assurance Graduate to Project Quality Manager. In 2010, she won a Henley Business School Bursary Award in the "Women in Business" category of an MBA Executive Programme competition in UK, but decided not to accept at the last minute in order to move to Australia.

Inspired by what's possible when working with people rather than processes, she left her well-paid career in QA and moved to Australia to start again as a facilitator and trainer. Since then, she has worked for an Australia's largest independent oil and gas supplier as a specialist facilitator and trainer. She runs workshops with dozens of internal decision makers, external companies, and community representatives. More recently, Iwona founded Red Hot Bananas workshops, including a highly successful Business Master Class that brings dozens of small businesses together with experienced business people.

She is a member of Australian Asian Facilitator's Network group and the International Association of Facilitators. Since March 2015, she's been coordinating the IAF Perth chapter. In May 2016, Iwona became a Certified Professional Facilitator (CPF) through the International Association of Facilitators (IAF).

Iwona lives in Perth with her very supportive partner, Austin. With their first baby on the way, she is looking forward to the challenges ahead and to spending more time enjoying life.

For more information about Iwona's workshops and educational programs, please visit www.iwonapolowy.com.

AUSTIN WILSON

Austin was born in Manchester, UK to his Dutch mother and Irish father. Growing up, he participated in a number of sports and swam competitively until his late twenties. He soon learnt the value of discipline, commitment, and, most importantly, delayed gratification! After completing his degree in chemical engineering, he started his career as a Plant Superintendent with the largest international oil and gas company in the UK. The industry has taken him to work in various places around the world, where he has worked on many complex world-class oil and gas developments.

Austin has worked hard to educate himself, reading countless books, attending seminars, doing sports and art and just giving things a go. He had a number of business successes beyond his ordinary work, including Database Design and Property Investment.

When standing as a president of CASM (Contemporary Artists Surrealist Movement), he employed his partner Iwona to facilitate a Strategic Planning workshop for his club. He was stunned to see what was possible through the use of only one facilitated workshop, and he loved the energy created in the room that helped the Artists get together, create a vision for the future, and clear a pathway forward. Since then, he has become passionate about empowering Iwona to complete this series of books, as he truly believes facilitation does make a difference for people working well together.

Austin lives in Perth with his lovely partner Iwona, anticipating his new life adventures as a dad, which inspires him to be the best he can be each and every day.

###